Beds

"It was such
a lovely day,
I thought
it was a pity
to get up."

W. Somerset Maugham

Beds

Diane Von Furstenberg

Photographs by Stewart O'Shields

Design by B.W. Honeycutt

Produced by Olivier Gelbsmann

Bantam Books

New York · Toronto · London · Sydney · Auckland

BEDS

A Bantam Book / November 1991

Library of Congress Cataloging-in-Publication Data

Von Furstenberg, Diane.
Beds/Diane Von Furstenberg: photographs by Stewart O'Shields.
p.   cm.
Includes bibliographical references.
ISBN 0-553-07195-5
1. Beds. 2. Bedrooms. 3. Sleeping customs. 4. Interior decoration.
I. Title.
GT3000.5.B44V66 1991
392'.36—dc20   91.9397 CIP

Published simultaneously in the United States and Canada

Bantam Books are published by Bantam Books, a division of Bantam Doubleday
Dell Publishing Group, Inc. Its trademark, consisting of the words "Bantam Books"
and the portrayal of a rooster, is Registered in U.S. Patent and Trademark Office
and in other countries. Marca Registrada, Bantam Books, 666 Fifth Avenue,
New York, New York 10103.

Printed in Italy by New Interlitho S.p.A. - Milan
0 9 8 7 6 5 4 3 2 1

To my mother, Lily.

Acknowledgments

It has been an exciting journey creating this book, one that involved many stops in many homes, many people speaking many different languages. While the languages may have been different, the ceremonies were all quite similar—all so very gracious. It is difficult to ask people to reveal to the camera such an intimate and private part of their lives. But the responses to our calls, often coming on the spur of the moment or late at night, were always kind and generous. I cannot thank enough all those who opened their doors to us—including those who, for reasons of space, could not be included in the final version.

Photographing the beds in these homes was such a personal experience. When we arrived on the threshold of the bedroom, seeing the bed for the first time, it was as though the bed were surrounded by a pocket of silence, within which could be heard the delicate heartbeat of an individual lifestyle. This commanded a great deal of respect, and therefore, I tried in each case to honor the presentation of the bed as it was upon our arrival. It is my sincere hope that this collection of portraits will reflect the enthusiasm that we experienced during our work on the project.

Getting the book off the ground would not have been possible without the help of the following. First and foremost, I would like to thank my friend Olivier Gelbsmann. I have been able to rely on him to follow up on my most fleeting suggestions, to maintain open lines of communication, and to scout and organize action on an international scale. His patience, determination, and supreme sense of style have made the entire project fruitful.

Stewart O'Shields has devoted boundless energy and superb talent to realizing this project, following me around the world with heavy equipment to create a beautiful collection of photographs. Many sincere thanks also to Antoine Meyer and Massimo Listri for their excellent photographic contributions.

My deepest gratitude to Coleen O'Shea for her invaluable guidance and for keeping us clearly on track; to Becky Cabaza and Linda Biagi at Bantam for their great assistance; to B. W. Honeycutt for his enthusiasm and artistic talent; to Richard Bernstein, Michele Rubin, Geoffrey Freitag, Madison Cox, John Jay, Kirsty Kröner, Konstantine Kakanias, and Kelly Morris, who so generously invested their personal time, skill, and talent to help make this book possible; to Angela Miller for her friendly advice; and to many friends, friends of friends, artists, decorators, architects, antique dealers, writers, stylists, designers, and all the

"Sleep,
my little one,
sleep,
my pretty one,
sleep."

Alfred, Lord Tennyson

other gifted people who listened to us and responded so generously.

Thanks to: Mrs. Primrose Bordier, Mr. Pietro Cicognani, Mrs. Beatrice Cifuentes-Sarmiento, Miss Gloria Cohen, Mrs. Marilyn Evins, Mr. Dino Franzin, Prince Egon von und zu Furstenberg, Mrs. Sabrina Gismondi, Mrs. Florence Grinda, Miss Geraldine Grinda, Ms. Annabelle D'Huart, Mr. Dakota Jackson, Ms. Amy Kassak, Mr. Olivier Lefuel, Mr. Peter Marino, Mr. Robert Metzger, Mr. Daniel Meyer, Mr. J. G. Mitterand, Ms. Sarah Montaigue, Ms. Sandra Nunnerley, Mr. Marc Ostier, Mr. Patrick Ourcade, Ms. Manuela Papatakis, Mr. Franco Pianon, Ms. Patricia Piva, Mr. Howard Rosenman, Mr. Ettore Sottsass, and Mrs. Nicole Wisniak.

And without the following people, who welcomed us into their homes and allowed us to approach the precious world of their dreams, there would be no book at all: Mrs. Mona Ackerman, Senatore Suni Agnelli, Mrs. Nicole Altero, Mr. and Mrs. Paul Auduis, Count Balthazar Klossowski de Rola, Mr. J. P. Beaujard, Princess Minnie de Beauvau Craon, Ms. Marisa Berenson, Mrs. D. Dixon Boardman, Mr. Mattia Bonetti, Mr. Fernando Botero, Count Brando and Countess Brandolini D'Adda, Countess Ruy Brandolini D'Adda, Baroness Roger de Cabrol, Mrs. Madeleine Castaing, Mr. François Catroux, Ms. Stephanie Cauchoix, César, Countess Marina Cicogna, Mr. and Mrs. Francesco Clemente, Mr. and Mrs. Asher Edelman, Mr. Jimmy Etro, Mrs. Barbara Del Vicario Foscari, Mr. Vincent Fourcade, Prince Alexandre von und zu Furstenberg, Princess Tatiana von und zu Furstenberg, Count Rofredo Gaëtani, Mr. Valentino Garavani, Ms. Elizabeth Garouste, Mr. and Mrs. Joel Goldfarb, Mr. Jacques Grange, Prince Michael and Princess Marina of Greece, Mr. Mark Hampton, Mrs. Nancy Stoddart Huang, Mr. Stephan Janson, Mr. Jed Johnson, Mr. and Mrs. Mick Jones, Miss Nathalie Karg, Mr. and Mrs. Calvin Klein, Mr. and Mrs. Thadee Klossowski, Mrs. Françoise Lafon, Mr. Karl Lagerfeld, Mr. Kenneth Jay Lane, Mrs. Hilda Langolon, Mr. Hilton McConnico, Ms. China Machado, Mrs. Elena Marchi, Ms. Jane Millet, Mr. Teddy Millington Drake, Lord Jamie Neidpath, Duchess of Northumberland, Countess Clara Agnelli Nuvoletti, Mr. and Mrs. Carlos Pagani, Mr. Umberto Pasti, Mr. Izhar Patkin, Count Dino and Countess Pecci Blunt, Avvocato Carlo Pecora, Mrs. Giselle Michard Pelissier, Mr. Johnny Pigozzi, Mrs. Andrée Putman, Mrs. Elena Quarestone, Count and Countess Jean de Rohan Chabot, Baron and Baroness Eric de Rothschild, Baroness Guy de Rothschild, Mr. and Mrs. Kenny Scharf, Mrs. Jacqueline Schnabel, Mr. Julian Schnabel, Countess Sharon Sondes, Mr. John Stefanidis, Mr. Perucho Valls, Mr. Ed Victor, Baroness Gérard de Waldner, Baron Thilo von Watzdorf, Mr. and Mrs. Jann Wenner, Lord Weymouth, and Mrs. Priscilla Rattazzi Whittle.

Additional thanks to: Adirondack Museum (Adirondack Historical Society), New York; Château de Fontainebleau, France; Château de Haroué, France; Château de Malmaison, France; Hancock Shaker Village, Inc., Massachusetts; HG (The Condé Nast Publications, Inc.), New York City; Lannan Foundation, Los Angeles; Longleat House, England; Metropolitan Home (Meredith Corporation), New York City; The Metropolitan Museum of Art, New York City; Monticello, home of Thomas Jefferson (The Thomas Jefferson Memorial Foundation), Virginia; The Museum of Modern Art, New York City; National Gallery of Canada, Ottawa; Musée National de Palais de Compiègne, France; Palazzo Pisani Moretta, Italy; Peggy Guggenheim Collection, Venice; Service Photographique de la Réunion des Musées Nationaux, Paris; Syon House, England; Villa Foscari (Malcontenta), Italy; Villa Medici, Rome; Virginia Museum of Fine Arts, Virginia; Vogue (The Condé Nast Publications, Inc.).

Lighting equipment for Stewart O'Shields courtesy of Balcar Techno, New York City.

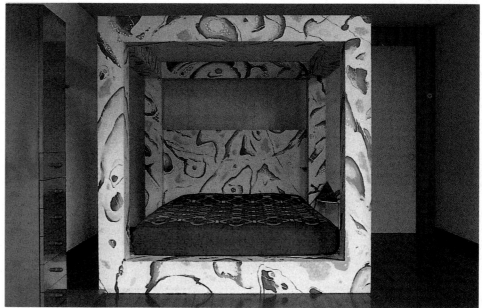

Beds

"Early to bed and early to rise, makes a man healthy, wealthy, and wise."

Benjamin Franklin

"To all,
to each,
a fair goodnight,
And pleasing
dreams,
and slumbers
light."

Sir Walter Scott

I remember

when I was a child, my mother would say the very same words before going to bed every night: "I bless the soul who invented the bed." Through her little tradition, I developed a deep appreciation for the nightly ritual of getting into bed. I slept in those years in a very delicate Louis XVI bed, decorated by a beautiful fabric with a yellow stripe and tiny roses, positioned alongside a wall displaying my guitar and favorite record covers. In the darkness, as my sheets gradually returned more of my own warmth to me, I felt so grateful for this chance to commune with myself—to reflect on my day, on my future and past, until sleep took over. In every way, my bed was where I was brought closer and closer to myself.

As I grew up, it was in various school beds that I truly realized that my bed was my home. In a room shared with others, there was one space I didn't share: the bed. And so by surrounding it with cherished personal objects, I made it my very own home. It reminds me now of the child's game of "making a tent" out of his or her bed, turning what is already the most personal part of the house into an even more private "home"—a home within a home within a home, unfolding like Chinese boxes.

Even today, I am thankful for the communion that going to bed brings. My children, whenever I am away, have always loved to "borrow" my bed. And in turn, anytime I visit my father in his home in Belgium, he invariably offers me his bed. Even for an adult, there is an incomparable feeling of security being in the cocoon of a parent's bed.

The simple word itself, "bed," is so full of evocations. During the course of

"In bed my real
love has always
been the sleep
that rescued me
by allowing me to
dream."

Luigi Pirandello

preparing this book, I saw how warm, how personal and disarming a word it is: each time I told anyone of my subject matter, beds, the word would inevitably elicit a smile.

To do a book on the subject of beds seemed inevitable. Since beds reflect life and life is a journey, here, then, is a journey through beds. There seems to be no more personal a reflection of the self than one's bed. Each page is in a sense the voyeur, opening the door, hopefully to discover the intimate universe of the one person who owns that bed.

Looking at beds, which of course have been with us throughout time, we see how life used to be lived and expressed, and how it is lived today. Originally just a gathering of dry leaves covered by an animal skin, beds eventually became an opportunity for pharaohs, emperors, and kings to express power and distinction. Many of the world's most gifted cabinetmakers, architects, artists, and artisans were commissioned to create truly extraordinary beds; and so they give us an opportunity to view some of the best craftsmanship by some of the finest talents through the centuries. Many of these beds appear in today's homes in settings outside the bedroom, reflecting a contemporary lifestyle, in which things happen faster, and more activities fill a single day. These changes have led to a new, broader view of the functions a bed can serve.

This collection is intended as a portrait of the bed, evoked through a series of "still life" photographs of some of the most exceptional and distinguished beds to be found throughout the world. Brought together in all their diversity, these beds awaken the imagination, asking it to fill in the space between one bed and the next with fantasy. Perhaps, as it is in dreams, it is in the sudden shift from one scene to the next that one's deepest, most fundamental emotions lie. In this drifting state, hovering between one example and the next, one is lulled into the relaxing, endless comfort of an ideal world—a perfect bed of the imagination.

Beds are the place to experience moments for which words are inappropriate…for hour upon hour of speechless sleep, colored only by indescribable dreams. Having grown past the age for "making tents," we can always appreciate that growing sense of warmth as the bed brings us through each shrinking box, ever closer to ourselves.

the miracle of infancy is captured in the dazzling bird's-eye maplewood crib from the Paris collection of Marcel Grunspan. Detailed with the gilded bronze swans of the Imperial family and suspended by chains, the cradle seems to float in the air.

Beds Throughout Life

or each one of us, for each person at every age, there is a bed, a place that is harbor to our most intimate of moments...our moments of abandon.

The cradle has always symbolized the dawn of a new life. Ready before birth, it expresses all the hope and passion of love and of lovers. The center of their joy, it holds sway in the bedroom, a nest of pink or blue. Occupied for several months or several years, it is then tucked away in an attic where it patiently awaits a new birth. Then brought down, cleaned, and renewed, it resumes its place of honor.

Bigger and without the wooden bars of the crib, the child's bed reflects a budding independence. It is easy for the child to climb in and as easy for him to fall out. The child feels less as if he were in a nest and more as if he might take flight. He doesn't like to go to bed at night, and he likes leaving it even less in the morning. Drifting toward sleep, during those long moments that seem to last an eternity, he stares at the shadows playing on his walls and windows, by turns frightened and reassured. The sights seen from this bed and the sounds that surround it become a most valued and cherished memory. Imagination, fear and love, cries and laughter—all inhabit this first landscape of childhood. A place of dreams and nightmares, the bed is a refuge, a secret dwelling, and sometimes an impregnable fortress. The most beautiful of moments are those the child shares with his mother who provides comfort, with his father who tells a story, or with another child who spends the night. He jumps up and down on it, discovering the pleasure of flight, the glee of pillow fights, and the enthusiasm of Indian tent games. Throughout it all, the bed remains a shelter

during chicken pox, sore throats, and fevers. The covers protect, the sheets are cool, the light swirls, and the child falls asleep, overcome with fatigue.

The bed of solitude is that of the adolescent. It is a bed that witnesses innumerable frustrations, a place where one's senses are awakened, the yearning for company one moment, solitude the next. It is the bed of first dreams and first disappointments, of love and whispered confidences, the place where one finds oneself alone, sad, and misunderstood, confiding in the childhood teddy bear. It is a bed where one might read, write, study, or simply daydream. Youth is the epoch of idols. Their photos and posters decorate the walls: rock singers and baseball players, actors and philosophers. One goes to sleep dreaming of becoming Marilyn, Madonna, or Albert Einstein.

The first bed of love is rarely a premeditated one. It is a bed of passion and of promise. It is an unexpected bed, a bed of adventure, a memory for life.

The young adult's bed often consists of a mattress on the floor. Scattered cushions and books reflect an untidy life, a life of early efforts, of first success and sometimes failure. It is a bed that shelters those frightening moments of love, so full of life and hope.

The bed of newlyweds is large, sumptuous, and

the First Bed: This dainty French antique baby's bed, graced by a hand-painted folk
art motif, captures the innocence of childhood. Photo by Antoine Meyer.

In the busy center of New York City, the nursery room of Baroness Roger de Cabrol is a nest of warmth and love for the newborn baby. Blankets, toys, and soft fabrics envelop the child's sleep and playtime, while a music box's sweet songs fill the air. A classic wooden cot and family chest filled with toys complete this nursery, truly a safe haven for baby, above left.

a traditional American pinewood headboard is glimpsed behind a child's toy box of treasures, above right.

In the spacious room of a New York residence, a truly exceptional bi-level twin bed provides the ultimate sleeping place for children. Designed by Peter Marino and carved in massive pinewood, it provides both the comfort of company and, with its sheltering drapes, the privilege of privacy. Matching blue and white comforters complete the look. At once practical and decorative, this modern design in a classic room will provide joy to the childhood years of many generations, left.

omnipotent. Created with great attention to detail, its sheets are chosen with scrupulous care, embroidered, and perfumed. In the days of kings and queens this bed was at the center of the castle, a sacred place, where future dynasties were conceived and born. For others, the nuptial bed is often in a hotel. It is a bed that is borrowed, but which keeps all its importance, the memory as the bed of the first night.

And then there is the matrimonial bed, the bed that symbolizes the achievement of love, the bed for first arguments; for lazy, intimate breakfasts; for conception, pregnancy, television, reading—and even family picnics. It's a bed that evolves and protects the family unit. It changes as the years pass and tastes alter. It's a bed that has been designed, decorated; an almost perfect reflection of the couple that inhabits it. Sometimes it splits into two, becoming twin beds, or per-

haps it takes on separate personalities, one feminine, the other masculine. As the beds separate, so do lives, becoming individual once again.

There are also temporary beds. Anonymous beds, where one stays and then leaves: hospital, hotel, or guest beds. They are witnesses to various conditions of life. And then there are beds in trains, which draw one to sleep, lulled by the whir and spark of wheels and tracks. There are the luxurious, rocking beds of cruise liners and even the bumpy beds of airplanes. These beds that move are clouds, flying carpets, that sweep one away toward unseen horizons.

The light dims and the bed becomes the place of final wisdom. As one dreams that last dream, that those one loved will be blessed, the bed, witness to the most intimate of moments, remains silent in the room, awaiting a new beginning.

this stunningly simple iron bed is inspired by a Napoleon I campaign bed. Its graceful, sculptured contours are surrounded by the intriguing trompe l'oeil decor. This fine piece of craftsmanship was designed by artist Julian Schnabel for his daughter.

ettore Sottsass designed this striking bed for a young boy. In the classic and trendy Italian city of Milano, this design combines the country's sense of old nobility with the city's changing industrial fortunes and latest fashion edge. With clean and daring lines and pure, sleek cobalt-blue colors, this is indeed a contemporary retreat.

a young girl's place to dream combines elements of the old and the new with this house-within-a-house motif. The pinewood bed with curves rests near the life-size dollhouse, which also functions as a partition between this bedroom and another. Favorite pinups, teenage pinks and purples, and an antique quilt make this a daughter's charming hideaway.

the young son of musician Mick Jones has a boy's wish come true in this bedroom filled with masculine touches. Surrounding the simple wood frame are reflections of sport in the soccer ball and sneakers, and reflections of music in the guitar. This living space is a fine melding of interests for any son.

15

a *young gentleman's room, designed by Peter Marino, is created around this gracious iron-frame bed. Dramatically decorated with its darker colors and green and blue tartan order, this is a soothing place to sleep or study, ideal for a single student who comes home to reflect on the day's adventures.*

a *cream and indigo* toile *de Jouy creates a romantic enclosure filled with light and space, accented by the draped antique lace and upholstered, toile-covered crown. The fabric design, "La Villageoise," is by Brunschwig & Fils. Inspired by a lit à la polonaise, this room, designed by Nancy Stoddart Huang, is filled with the early wishes of a young woman.*

i *n Paris, interior designer Stephanie Cauchoix designed this Gallic dreamscape, dominated by the Portuguese black-lacquered bed. The relaxed distraction of country living is offset by the dramatic dark wood and accented by the Provincial-style curves of the bed frame. Ochre-striped wallpaper highlights the drapery of Indonesian yellow fabric, lined with an off-white antique fabric cascading around the head of the bed. The baldaquin is draped inside with white embroideries from St. Gallen, France, and printed silk by Thorp of London. The outside drapery is an Indonesian batik with an added border. The quilt is an antique, bought in Brighton, England.*

at the Venice country residence of Countess Clara Agnelli Nuvoletti is a room graced by a young girl's bed, looking like a scene from a Mozart opera. The house is placed within the magic of a beautiful garden, and the inside bedroom reflects this. With the charm of a romantic libretto, the draped canopy bed creates a beguiling feeling of privacy and solitude.

the SoHo loft and gallery of Nathalie Karg in New York is a place for both work and pleasure. The walls display artwork, while a futon creates a work and living environment. The room's horizons seem to stretch to the edge of the city. The blue Lucite table, at the head of the futon, by French designer Yves Klein, adds to a room which breathes with both energy and peace.

In the south of France, Johnny Pigozzi mixes business with pleasure in this witty bedroom designed by Ettore Sottsass. A smattering of male pursuits fills the area surrounding the bed, whose design is simple and stylish. A view into a man's world that is filled with both humor and work, this room shows that all enjoyments can be relished equally.

a *city for lovers, Venice boasts the dazzling Gritti Palace hotel, in which the romantic honeymoon suite is a nuptial retreat with a view to the world below. It is a place for creating unforgettable memories of love and celebration to return to again and again. Secluded for privacy for two, the room overlooks the Grand Canal below. The canal is a gentle reminder of the world outside without disturbing the intimacy of the honeymoon suite.*

the ancient and
fine art of lace-
making is exhibited
in the exquisite
bedsheet and covers
of these Jesurum
delicacies. One
of the most
extraordinary
places to choose
exceptional linens,
Jesurum was
founded in Venice
in 1870, and still
maintains the
distinguished work
of its past with
antique and
modern lace, hand-
painted motifs, and
rare detail. The
handcrafted nature
of these bed
accessories makes
each a unique rest-
place and treasured
trousseau.

an intimate feeling of the Romantic period marks the master
bedroom of Ann Jones. Textures seem to carry on a quiet
conversation around the sleeper, as the puckered bedspread is
countered by the ruffles and drapes in their pastel shades,
and the strong wrought iron of an art deco torchère floor lamp
fills the room with a quaint light. Fabrics by English designer
Zandra Rhodes.

inside the New York town house of Rolling Stone *magazine*
founders Jann and Jane Wenner, the confident curves of this art
deco–style bed exude a sleek and daring modernism. Carved of
bird's-eye maple wood, the bed was created by art deco designer
Pierre Chareau circa 1930.

actress Marisa Berenson can drift on a cloud of meditative and spiritual dreams in this peaceful setting in her Paris apartment. Slumbers of gold and lace are guarded by the visionary painting of Madonna and Child at the head, while the fabric drapes open like the curtain on a theater's first night. In Paris, where "trade is art and art's philosophy" (Elizabeth Barrett Browning), this bed combines the practicalities and desires of both. Photo by Antoine Meyer.

designed by François Catroux, this bedroom in the Paris home of Baroness Sylvia de Waldner is a reclusive nest for gold-washed slumber. The four-poster bed is tented with Indian design–inspired fabrics and an upholstered headboard. Eclectic touches of art enhance the settled, cushioned richness of the surroundings. Photo by Antoine Meyer.

a *breath of very French air rustles through the sumptuous elegance of this room in the Paris residence of Giselle Michard Pelissier, designed by Christian Badin and Stephanie Cauchoix. The chintz fabric, from Mrs. Monroe of London, is a poem, luxurious and seductive, and mixes gracefully with the four-poster drape canopy lit à la polonaise and its gingham silk-taffeta lining in green and pink.*

the Duchess bed at Syon House, located near London, displays classic English elegance brought to life with this high canopy bed, trimmed with carved flowers and graced with fine antique bed linens. The George III bed is a mahogany four-poster with a painted serpentine corniche, adorned with carved white scrollwork. The English love of garden details and pleasantry speaks in the simple hand-painted chairs and bed-carvings motif.

designer John Stefanidis owns this very English four-poster, eighteenth-century bed, which graces a room in his London home. With its high canopy, draped with a champagne taffeta, a sense of enclosure and rest is preserved with a mood of light and motion styled with fabric. A chaise longue rests at the foot of this scene of British elegance and simplicity.

an English George III mahogany bed provides the focal point of this room in the New York residence of Mark Hampton. This polychrome covered four-poster is draped with champagne silk from Scalamandre. The antique bed linens are from the collection of Mrs. Hampton

In a New York master bedroom, the evocative drama of the turn of the century is dramatically stated in this French antique bleached-wood bed, circa 1910. Its opulent lines are matched with antique lace bed linens from Alice's Antiques of New York City.

Just a half hour from the busy center of Paris is a discreet, charming country retreat, Verrières-le-Buisson, the year-round residence of interior designer Agnès Comar. The sleek Louis XVI military campaign bed stands nobly in the center of the room. The canopy bed is stretched with a hand-painted fabric in a single striped pattern, inspired by an eighteenth-century document. The fabric and the elegant, brushed-steel frame lend a masculine accent to this graceful room. A few pale and muted colors have been added to this delicate palette. The morning light embraces the room, giving life to all of its rare objects. The blanket and love seat coverings, bedsheets, pillowcases, and window draperies are all designed by Agnès Comar, Paris.

In designer Stephan Janson's home in Milano, this room is an exotic and stylish bedroom setting with an air of nonchalance and personal elegance. The bed is an open design, like an empty nomadic carriage. The blanket, topped with lustrous Indian brocade pillows, is from Marrakesh. The wrought iron baldaquin Lucca bed, circa 1820, is painted aubergine. The nineteenth-century draperies are from Bukhara.

In the New York bachelor pied-à-terre of former light-heavyweight boxing champion of Italy Count Roffredo Gaetani, the owner has surrounded the eighteenth-century baroque bed with the noble objects of his family inheritance: a bronze bust of Pope Bonifacio VIII, an ancestor, and a seventeenth-century tapestry adorned with the family crest.

In Paris, on the top floor of her boutique, the self-styled Empress of Art, Madeleine Castaing, has a reclusive retreat from the foibles of the present day. Antique-ivory bed linens and walls done in green freeze in time the dazzling glory of old elegance and history. With its nostalgic nuances, this room is lit with the remembrance of things past.

diane Von Furstenberg's bedroom retreat in her Paris apartment is designed by François Catroux. A campsite for a nomadic traveler to rest and plan, this bed is a tented fantasy come true for the restless and restless at heart. Draped in ivory-striped satin, this is the place to come home to at journey's end, where the gypsy journeyer is queen of all she surveys. Bed linens by Porthault. Photo by Antoine Meyer.

"**r**ome! Niobe of nations, the orphans of the heart shall turn to thee!" So said Lord Byron. Senatore Suni Agnelli requires both home and office in a city where it is possible to combine work with style. A self-contained realm with a view to the world outside, this is a room in which the bed, an Empire bird's-eye maple, invites both rest and work.

a *touch of
Victoriana and the
days of the Raj is
present in this
gentleman's room
belonging to
designer Kenneth
Jay Lane. The
bed, centered to
command the room,
rests below the
canopy like a jewel
in a crown. The
cool, masculine
lines are
complemented by
the rich, sapphire-
green tones and
exotic tiger skin,
which are
reminiscent of the
alluring East.*

true elegance can be found in this New York apartment designed by Peter Marino. It's easy to forget the noise and the city outside in the sparkling and cool white-lacquered enclosure with its two potier-*like French doors framing the bed. A fabric-covered wall in pink-and-white-checked gingham silk creates a feeling of relaxed gracefulness. This is a refreshing and dazzling room.*

Count Brando Brandolini D'Adda's Paris home houses this Louis XVI bed. Signed by cabinetmaker Jacob, it is decorated by Renzo Mongiardino with fabrics by Braquenie. This fine piece is a rare treasure and a luxurious nest in which to sleep.

luxurious travel by train is a romantic fantasy shared by all who live for the journey. This train travel-car is reminiscent of the more elegant, civilized age of the Orient Express from London to Istanbul, though it travels from Washington to Chicago. Combining themes from both East and West with a fin de siècle air of opulence, this travel-car provides a gentle buffer between the intrigues of old-time train travel and the comfort of contemporary travel. Courtesy American European Express Railway Train Deluxe.

away from Paris, Rome, and New York on his yacht, the T.M.B. Blue One, Roman couturier Valentino Garavani retires to the solid lines of this room, decorated by Peter Marino. The white-lacquered bed reflects the stark freshness of the sea air, broken by an accent of navy blue with a cashmere throw blanket, and anchored by a dhurrie wool carpet custom-woven by Van Besouw in Holland. It captures hints of an old-time Colonial elegance in a new spirit. Courtesy HG. Copyright 1989 by Condé Nast Publications. Photo by Nicolas Bruant.

the room in which Oscar Wilde died "beyond his means," in his own words, is a sumptuous and luminous room of dark baroque colors and witty touches of the dandy. The heavy, masculine bed and warm woods are lush and, though it was death Wilde met here, the room speaks of a life most fully loved. To rent the room today at Paris's L'Hôtel is to feel the world in which Wilde wrote and flourished.

business and pleasure strike a perfect harmony in this hotel room at the Royalton in New York. Philippe Starck created this sleek design, marked by nautical curves and a spare sophistication. Simple details demonstrate a superb quality, with the bed dressed by the finest of duvet covers and guest pillows. The room is pure, simple, yet romantically elegant, asserting a forward-thinking approach to the tradition of the hotel visit.

in the heart of New York's theater district, the jazz-tinged vitality of this hotel room in the Paramount suggests the neon diversity waiting just outside. The playful Philippe Starck design frames a stark bed with the warm classicism of Vermeer's ''The Lacemaker,'' a work whose warmth and intimacy become almost explosive in this sleek and cinematic context. The room's theatrical originality truly marks the next generation of hotel rooms.

antiquarian Nicole Altero combines the charm and wistfulness of the past with the comfortable delights of the present in this Paris attic guest room. The collapsible military campaign bed is offset by the delicate floral coverings. The light from the skylight pours through to the evergreen leaf pattern carpet.

breakfast in bed
is a relaxed luxury
at the country
farmhouse of Diane
Von Furstenberg,
surrounded by a
porcelain blue and
white antique
American quilt and
bed linens designed
by Diane Von
Furstenberg.
Sunlight streams
through the
windows and the
air is fragrant
with flowers.

Beds for All Seasons

Chapter 2

The bed is the natural focus of a bedroom. Therefore, great attention should be paid to the type of bed that is selected, the place it is given, and the way it is adorned.

Throughout the ages, many beliefs and superstitions have surrounded the subject of the bed. Its position in the room is often an especially great concern. Several theories as old as antiquity recommend that the head should face north, and the foot south. The ancient Chinese science of Feng Shui, the study of magnetic fields and geobiology, reveals that a badly placed bed can cause discomfort and sickness.

A host of other recommendations have been inspired by the subject of the bed's environment. These include keeping the bed at a distance from any pieces of metal, magnetic material, water pipes, or electrical wires; avoiding intense humidity, or heat that is too strong or too dry; and minimizing materials that produce a lot of dust.

The bed is a place to dream, to reflect, to build an imagined future, to remember. The more space around it—the more freedom, air, and openness—the better. It is a strategic point, a nerve center: the telephone, papers, pens—all of the tools of daily life should be at hand.

Selecting a bed is always a personal choice, the marriage of aesthetic and practical considerations. As decorative furniture, it can be a symbol of self-image, character, and personality. Comfort and health must also be addressed, starting with a good foundation—be it a box spring or platform. A good mattress should be firm, but still have a certain elasticity in order to support the spine. It should be able to absorb moisture and allow it to evaporate, to maintain a proper temperature so the

the guest room in the Watermill, Long Island, countryside home of China Machado is a quiet, nostalgic trip into the elegance of the past. The walls are covered with antique blue and white toile de Jouy, and the old-fashioned brass beds are covered with matching fabric. This is a complete suite with bath for total privacy.

skin can breathe and the blood circulate. There are mattresses of coconut fiber, sisal, wool, and cotton; but the best of the natural fibers is horsehair, particularly the horsehair from cold climates like that of Argentina. The long ends of the tail are cut, spun, and plaited to create a maximum of elasticity. There is no more precious padding than horsehair, though one unique mattress is the Simmons Beautyrest. Its individually pocketed coils allow great comfort

and support of the body.

A bed lends itself to such a range of decorative treatments that it can give an entire room a very distinct atmosphere. It is impractical to change the decor of a room—the wallpaper or furniture or draperies—with every change of season; but by focusing on the bed, a very potent effect can be obtained.

Through styling, a single room can create the feeling of any climate. It might give the sense that a rich, shady redwood forest or a lush tropical

everglade is just outside the window. Or it might suggest a cabin in the Adirondacks, a beach house by the sea, a snowy ski lodge, or a ranch in a New Mexico desert.

Treat the seasons as an inspiration. Let them influence the choice of bedsheets and covers, textures, colors, and styling touches. The current season can be reflected using this palette; but always feel free to re-create the mood of one season, even in the midst of another, through the styling of the bed and its

surroundings.

Spring might inspire the use of pastel colors, a desire to bring a sense of freshness into the air with tulips or flower buds—real or, if necessary, artificial—or the distinctively springtime scent of lilac. If a masculine mood is desired, the look of the bed clothing might be more tailored, a Brooks Brothers style using mostly whites and blues, wide stripes or pinstripes. A feminine look could be more adventurous in its array

Pauline Boardman's New York home has a springtime setting awash in rose-pink silk. Soft and enveloping, the canopy bed with an upholstered headboard is a cozy escape from the demands of New York City. The outside fabric is adapted by Brunschwig & Fils from documents found in the Paris Musée des Arts Décoratifs. The sheets are from Porthault. The inside canopy is lined with a pink and white ribbon silk fabric and is edged in pink and cream.

this campaign daybed with wheels serves as a guest bed, or simply a place for a friend to gaze out at the clouds over Paris in this city retreat of Diane Von Furstenberg. Warm, rich colors provide a comfortable welcome, as soothing as the lush folds of the blanket covering the night table. The bedsheets and pillows are burnt ochre and cypress green, with a blanket of burnt sienna. Shades of taupe and silver color the antique silk batik bed linens. All bedding and the table blanket are designed by Agnès Comar.

of colors and prints. It might include a blend of pastels, or a bold floral print, a scarf print, or even an animal print. Beautiful designer sheets are very fashionable in any season, of course, and it is hard to resist the urge to use them to make the bedroom a pampering, elegant environment.

In summertime, when the heat begins to swell and the sun rises earlier, more vivid colors may be apropos. With a selection of cool colors, the bed will be a respite from the heat; while dressed in floral prints, it will share a sense of the bounty and fertility of the season. For hot nights, linen sheets are cool and delightful: their natural fibers are a pleasure to the skin. While they do require the extra care of ironing, they're well worth it for the luxury they provide. Their distinctive off-white, creamy color also gives a sense of the old-fashioned, the turn of the century, when they were at their peak of

distinctive one-of-a-kind New York Leron linens create a look of casual elegance with hand-embroidered appliqué. Garlands of flowers and fleur-de-lis are reminders of a bygone era of luxury and style. The room is decorated, and the bed styled, by Sandra Nunnerley.

popularity. Fresh lavender sachet between the bedsheets will give a wonderful, flowery scent, while also helping to deter moths, and the fresh scent of cut flowers can fill a room. For the occasional cool night or a chilly summer rain, a wonderful summer cotton blanket can be kept on hand. To cover the bed, a light cotton bedspread from

Italy or an Indian silk bedcover adds an excellent touch to the room.

As the leaves turn, gorgeous colors emerge; the autumn air becomes crisp, tempting one to add weight and deep, rich colors to the bed. Autumn weather can be unpredictable, which makes a layering of blankets wise. An extra stack of blankets placed on a bedside chair is a

warming sight. To augment the rustic feeling of the room, try a beautiful Amish quilt or an American Indian antique blanket. Reflect the harvest season with dried leaves or gourds at the bedside. Eucalyptus is a wonderful, refreshing scent and sight for the fall, and has long been believed to have a therapeutic effect. Place several branches in a

the attic room in China Machado's country home offers overnight guests privacy and a rustic setting with dark, exposed beams and the cozy atmosphere of a cabin in the woods. Wide-planked pinewood floors with a throw rug and earth-color themes complement the open brick face and wood-burning stove.

dry bedside vase and activate the aroma every few days by gently brushing the hands upward along the leaves.

As the snowy season takes over, blankets satisfy the desire for warmth and comfort—be it a classic heavy wool blanket, a cashmere plaid from Scotland, or a guanaco fur blanket from Argentina. The same degree of warmth with a lighter, more summery weight can be obtained from a goosedown comforter. Change the color of the duvet cover to suit a variety of moods and occasions.

The festive air of the holiday seasons makes it enticing to experiment with stronger colors and exotic scents. Essential oils can be burned on light bulbs or candles, and a spicy scent enriches the atmosphere. It is always nice to light a scented candle or to fill the room with an aromatic spray. And a pomander in the linen closet is exquisite.

The seasons themselves need never restrict one's choice of bed clothing. It is the needs of the weather and the mood being expressed that take priority. A classical bed styling can be austere, impeccable; but the temptation to create a more seductive environment sometimes arises. Silk sheets, candlelight, luxurious textures, fragrances, and a soft and inviting look can all be given special attention. When we enter a room, the scent and the sight go hand in hand: we experience both immediately. Upon reaching the bed, we can touch its fabrics and textures before partaking of the full comfort and sensation to be had under its covers. Treat the bed as a piece of art. Put your heart into it, allow it to reflect your moods and sentiments. Whether it is the sleeping place for you, for a member of your family, or for your guests, it can be an expression of your caring, your love. The bedroom, year-round, can provide an experience to be savored.

a *summer English cottage in the enchanted gardens of Sissinghurst Castle in Kent displays an intriguing mix of old and new. Once the home of Vita Sackville-West, today it is a trip into a more elegant past. The early Italian Renaissance bed's rich elegance contrasts with the rustic, open brick face on the bedroom wall. The bed corners are highlighted with the carved figures of four women, an intriguing artistic accent.*

the Hamptons home of Kelly and Calvin Klein can welcome a guest to this secluded tower bedroom, highlighted in crisp navy blue and soothing white. With its brushed-iron canopy bed, this is simple, pure, and basic country style. The quilt is an antique and the bed linens are by Pratesi, right and below.

another guest room in the house by the sea relies on an Early American look of straightforward simplicity. The simple four-poster bed adds to its strictly elegant mood of form and function.

an ocean-view room in a Hamptons home lulls guests to sleep with this boat-shaped bed. Rocked by the sound of ocean waves and the smell of clean salt air through the open windows, the bed adds a nautical flair as the sun washes over this seaside room of Kelly and Calvin Klein.

high in the Chianti hills of Tuscany lies the country retreat of artist Teddy Millington Drake. The intoxicating fragrance of the rosemary bushes and the lavender fields wafts through the bedrooms' open windows, sweetening the air surrounding the Indian-styled four-poster beds, draped with the finest Indian cotton saris, above and right.

In Bahia, Brazil, mosquito netting is used not only for its summery look of sheer, open drapery, but also for its necessary use as a shield. Sun streams through and cuts equatorial slants of light across the bed, creating a mood for lazy dreaming.

This exotic setting features a tropical Balinese bed. A mood of endless summer is created with earthy wood tones accented by cool and protective mosquito netting. Flowers bloom in the open space, adding a hint of lazy sensuality to this island-style room. Photo by Antoine Meyer.

63

rich autumn spice colors combine with a
Southwestern flair, creating a Native
American/New Mexico style at home in
Connecticut. The warm hues and local folk-art
touches create an earthy desert mood.
Curios and collectibles add intriguing accents.

taking an uncomplicated approach to life, the
Shaker community dates back to England in 1747.
Shakers stress a separation from the material world
and are in some ways cousins of the Amish of
Pennsylvania. Their traditional lifestyle removes
them from luxury and modern dependencies. Self-
sufficient, they are well known for their unadorned
American Primitive-style furnishings and their
beautiful quilts and appliqués.

this 1905 American bed in the New York residence of interior designer Jed Johnson is done in an Egyptian manner. Its oak wood is decorated with fine polychrome detail, and dressed with an Egyptian appliqué bedspread from the eighteenth century. Desert tones of brush and sand are smooth complements to the dark, gracefully carved wood.

antiquarian designer Nicole Altero enjoys Chinese colonial style in Paris. The bed is of carved wood bamboos. These exotic bamboos and darker woods bring the mystery of old Shanghai into the bedroom.

In the Paris
residence of
Françoise Lafon,
an exotic Egyptian-
style decor prevails.
Spice colors and
shades of the
Sahara sands mix
with the carpet's
bold Nile turquoise.
The bed, with its
four posters carved
into regal lotus
blossoms, is painted
in the same hues,
melding into the
hieroglyphic
messages on the
hand-painted
walls. The striped
bed linens
embroidered with
gold thread are
designed by
Annabelle d'Huart
for Noël, Paris.

In a Venice palazzo, Pisani Moretta, furnishings grace this elegant bedroom. A Madonna and Child floats mystically above the double wooden beds. Deep woods and golden rose walls quietly illuminate the entire room in Renaissance light.

for winter in a private residence in Mexico City, a fur blanket creates a place for cozy relaxation while a painted sky lures the mind to dream. The antique character of this four-poster brass bed is highlighted by a collection of colonial art on an antique chest of drawers, in a surrounding which evokes a sense of both intimacy and openness. Photo by Massimo Listri.

Winter in Rome includes its share of cold nights, and in this Roman guest room in the home of Countess Marina Cicogna, a classic attic space becomes a warm and intimate refuge through its restrained elegance. Twin Napoleon III beds of antique brass and painted metal are guarded from the chill with cream-colored, featherweight duvet covers. Photo by Massimo Listri.

the mysterious atmosphere is as deep and rich as the aroma of incense in this guest bedroom in the New York residence of interior designer Vincent Fourcade. The English bed, dating from the 1860s, is of acajou wood and covered in silk damask fabrics, like the walls, by Tassinari and Chatel of France. Beneath the baldaquin, an eighteenth-century American orientalist painting adds an even deeper visual dimension.

this New York City penthouse designed by Nancy Stoddart Huang has a nineteenth-century–style master bedroom with a half-canopy king-sized bed and a damask, upholstered headboard wrapped with custom cording. The canopy panels and lining are from Clarence House and the rich bedspread is by Linda Fresco.

Japan's serene elegance is found in New York City at the home of artist Robert Homma. A futon, which is opened at night in the center of the room, creates order and harmony on all sides. Tatami mats and antique family linens are cool and full of peaceful grace. A Burmese Buddha gazes over the open and quiet space.

Countrified American coziness from the nineteenth century can be found in the rustic authenticity of this log cabin room at Bull Cottage in the Adirondack Museum. In bringing the outside natural world into the bedroom, a rural simplicity is achieved with warmth and charm. Sturdy woods and warm bedclothes, including an antique patchwork quilt, keep the harsher weather well away, but a pair of antique snowshoes over the bed are a reminder of the wintery world beyond the windows.

a cold-weather lodge in the Adirondacks is a winter wonderland. Warm, woodsy interiors are a cozy buffer against the outside chill. The bed is unbarked cedar with an asymmetrical headboard by Joseph O. A. Byers, made originally for his northern New York hotel, circa 1895. This is nineteenth- and early-twentieth-century backwoods charm in a snowy mountain hideaway found in the Adirondack Museum.

a *sumptuous bed is found in the Paris home of Prince Michael and Princess Marina of Greece. Rich royal colors, with a taste of Eastern flair, adorn the bed itself, topped with a mosquelike dome. This Louis XVI bed belonged to Madame du Barry. She managed to become the all-powerful favorite of Louis XV.*

Beds Outside the Bedroom

rdinarily, our beds are a matter of privacy. They are rarely seen by anyone outside the circle of those who are closest to us. And so when a bed moves out of its traditional environment, the bedroom, it invariably becomes a more aesthetic part of its new surroundings, interacting with the room in any number of ways.

As a visual centerpiece in a living space, the bed might inspire an especially elegant styling treatment: the finest of fabrics, a bountiful gathering of pillows, sensual drapings, or a surrounding collection of art. Or, depending on its design or its origins, the bed might by its very nature lend a new theme to the room. Perhaps it is an exotic bed, bringing a flavor of the Far East or the tropics into a country cottage or a city town house. It may add a sense of the visual grandeur of the past. Or it may simply raise to our consciousness those themes inherently linked to a bed: relaxation, luxury, fantasy, and romantic pursuits.

Such themes can immediately warm an unfamiliar guest. The bed in a living space is sending an understated message: It reminds us that at any moment we can, if we so choose, simply stretch out over its luxurious expanse and unwind.

The message that the bed sends can change, too, depending on the intimacy and familiarity of this guest. Early on in a courtship, the presence of a bed might create an awkward pressure—or it might provide an amusing private joke to mix with the body language and unspoken dynamics as the couple becomes acquainted.

an outstanding Napoleon I bed by Percier and Fontaine is a study in
elegant and stately power. Gilded bronzes recall the triumph of Napoleon's rule.
This setting is styled by François Catroux and is found in the collection of
Marcel Grunspan. Photo by Antoine Meyer.

For a more comfortable pairing, a conversation on a bed in a living room is like a conversation over champagne: a shared treat, an indulgence. It is as though the bed provides a doorway directly from the living space into the bedroom, allowing romance to progress without interruption.

The function of a bed outside the bedroom is far broader than the one inside the bedroom. A couch by day, it can be the bed of a favored houseguest at night. It can be the perfect place for an afternoon siesta, allowing us a lighter sleep that makes it easier to return to our routine—while in the luxury of the bedroom, we might be imperiled by the temptation to let our nap go on all day.

Beds can appear in the most accidental locations, or the most calculated....

Placed near the main entry of our residence, a bed provides our first welcome on returning home, the place where we throw down all our things—and perhaps, for a moment, ourselves.

Situated by a window, it is an irresistible recipe for daydreaming, lulling us with a freshening breeze and the play of light on trees or the clouds.

In a study, the bed is an ideal place to read, permitting the reader a range of relaxing positions as the story be-

In the study of Regina Edelman's New York retreat awaits this bed en bateau, circa 1800 Paris. Designed by brothers George Jacob (1768–1803) and Jacob Desmalter (1770–1851), its gilded bronze ornamentation includes torches tied by ribbon on the pilasters, and two delicate swans at the head, each holding a pearl necklace. A crowd of small pillows in panne velvet fabrics by Fortuny lightens the bed's solid lines. It is derived almost entirely from a bed created by the Jacob brothers for Madame Récamier.

comes by turn escapist, amusing, compelling, sensual, or suspenseful.

Sometimes, a bed will appear in a corridor or foyer, contradicting a space meant for flowing traffic with an invitation to linger in comfort.

On a terrace, where lounging is quite in order, the delightful twist is in the exotic luxury of sleeping in open air.

Then there are the beds that are not beds at all, but other pieces of furniture transformed by function into beds. The living room sofa, the divan, the couch, the chaise longue, the hammock—at times, these all can be alternative names for Bed.

The bed outside the bedroom makes apparent, more than any bed, the rich catalog of associations that the subject provokes. But more than anything, the bed outside the bedroom affords us added luxury. When the bedroom is just a bit too far away for convenience, the nearest bed available will do quite splendidly.

In Lord Jamie Neidpath's main drawing room beneath a great Jacobean plaster ceiling are twin Chinese Chippendale daybeds, covered with antique fabrics and pillows, and providing a focus for rest and conversation. Extremely elegant and graceful, this setting is found in Stanway, Gloucestershire, England.

a daybed in a Milano living room is a pure and elegant design that appears like an overture to the symphony that is the living room. A strawlike center adds form.

the bed of artist Jane Millet in Greenwich Village, fabricated of wrought iron, becomes the elegant center of the room, bringing the focus to the dramatic pieces of art done by Jane Millet herself. Cozy and eclectic, the room is full of experience in feeling and vision.

a*t the home of interior designer Perucho Valls, a silk satin-covered mattress
reveals the classical purity of the bed's essential simplicity and design.*

this Charles X bed in bird's-eye maple is in the bedroom of Alexandre von Furstenberg. Designed by Jean-Paul Beaujard, this is the look of a daytime couch transformed into a nighttime enclave of rest. The walls are covered with blue moiré fabrics. The cool blues create a soothing and harmonious effect. Bedding and wall fabrics are designed by Madeleine Castaing of Paris.

nestled within
the Greenwich
Village apartment
of designer Jane
Millet rests a
luminous oasis for
sleep and daytime
repose. Tucked into
an alcove like a
sunken bath with
nostalgic photographs
surrounding it, this
wrought iron sleigh
bed combines the
elements of easy
style bathed in
light pouring in
from the window.

In Reggio Emilia, Italy, the ascending corkscrew spirals of this carved four-poster bed inspire a highly decorative treatment, with a gathering of lustrous pillows covered in Indian brocade. Photo by Massimo Listri.

In the home of photographer Massimo Listri in Florence, Italy, the draping of elegant antique fabrics makes this Empire-period bed a space of decided repose and distinction. Photo by Massimo Listri.

In avvocato Carlo Pecora's Milano apartment, a bed rests in a red-cushioned alcove. The entire design is trompe l'oeil, including the bookshelves, creating a private, fantastical space for rest and work.

In interior designer Jacques Grange's Paris abode, a chaise longue is a graceful and comfortable touch in a relaxed study room.

the Paris home of Countess Georgina Brandolini D'Adda provides an opulent retreat with a Second Empire lit de salon *with rich fabrics. Decorated with gleaming inlaid mother-of-pearl, it is a flowered and romantic fantasy of the past. Photo by Antoine Meyer.*

this couch in the
New York study of
Kenneth Jay Lane
is resplendent in
amber and gold-
touched earth tones,
an enveloping,
pillowed place to
recline. The fabrics
are of antique
paisley. The look is
of a painting within
a painting, done
with Oriental
precision and detail.
Inviting and
sumptuous, it is a
place to nap or
carry on an
impassioned
courtship.

this nineteenth-century "Kang" opium bed in Hong-Mou wood from China is
a classic design. The headboard and the two sides are white and gray marble
inlaid plaques. Carvings of disks and crosses are done in the "Ju-i" style. The
spirit and sensuality of the Far East are expressed through color and design.
From the collection of C. T. Loo, Paris.

the mystique and primitive elegance of Africa can be found in Paris with this unusual African bed. The wood and earth colors of the savanna are evoked with the fabrics, while the designs themselves bring the secrets of Africa ever closer. Native sculpture finishes the effect of a haven in the jungle.

this is a daybed for an afternoon siesta. The tones of a Southwest desert are designed around minimal decor and are weathered, earthy, and mysterious. Bleached, natural wood and striped fabric from Portico in neutral colors are in keeping with the regional style, right .

this lounge chair from India is a casual hallway rest stop in clean and simple white, below.

teddy Millington Drake's Tuscan home is filled with all the scents and sights of the Italian countryside. Floral and herbal gardens satisfy the senses, and as the fragrant air drifts around the porch setting, the hills outside breathe the season's changes. The antique bench is covered with a cotton mattress, perfectly suited for a peaceful afternoon nap, right.

a *sleek iron sleigh bed designed for Jacqueline Schnabel by artist Julian Schnabel is accented by his overhanging modern painting. Old brocades and velvet pillows soften the spare headboard and open-frame style.*

Beds, Artists and Styles

leep and dreaming bring a kind of inspiration to every one of us. Surrounded by a sea of blankets, we wake sometimes still drifting, astonished at the vivid images we have just seen, the far reaches to which our minds have taken us during the night…surprised, that is, by our own imaginations.

For the artist, few resources are as vital as the imagination. While they have this in common, artists' beds can be as varied as the styles of their work.

"Life," said playwright Jean Anouilh, "is very nice, but it lacks forms. It is the aim of art to give it some." And so an artist might see the world through the capturing eye of the photographer, the interpretive eye of the painter, the dimensional sensitivity of the sculptor, the aesthetic sensitivity of the decorator, the spatial awareness of the architect, or the conceptual awareness of the writer. Or the artist may combine any of these talents, or those of still another art form—from dancing to fashion design or acting—to shape a very personal vision of the world.

Any of these talents might in turn shape the bed on which the artist chooses to sleep. The artist may take the bed as an opportunity to make a statement to the world, as Jayne Mansfield did with her lusty, pink silk, heart-shaped Hollywood starlet bed. The statement might instead be one of quiet despair, like the simple frame and mattress on which Marilyn Monroe left the world, or the bed in Van Gogh's famous painting—his sleeping place while recuperating in a sanitarium. Another, less deliberate kind of statement is made when there is no bed at all, just a simple pallet, as might be the case for the struggling artist.

To some, the bed offers an opportunity to create a shrine to

the painter Francesco Clemente's room is a place of uncomplicated peace with Asian grace and style. Minimal decor allows the artist's powerful painting overlooking the Japanese futon to command the room's space and mood.

the dream ritual, a salute to the playful unpredictability of our unconscious—the amusement park in our minds. Others prefer to retire to an austere, cleansing environment that will purify the mind with a Zen-like balance.

There is the artist's room that reflects a heightened appreciation of things aesthetic: beautiful materials, unique colors, distinctive motifs, a calming sense of proportion.

Or an artist might choose to be taken away by the bedroom environment, carried into another age by a Louis XV bed, or to another culture by a Japanese bed, or perhaps simply to the sea by a motif of oceanic decoration.

A single cherished theme can provide inspiration for other artists. For Jacques Grange, it is inspiration provided by the life of a single individual, Colette, a woman of compelling creativity herself. Following such a figure into the intriguing corners of her now-complete life must certainly provide rich resources for the mind to ponder and the imagination to re-create.

For Fernando Botero it is a theme on the order of myth, an "Ur" story, which soothes the jarring transition from sleep to wakefulness each morning. His voluptuous sculptures of the first human creators, Adam and Eve, dominate the foot of his bed, awaiting him, fertile with the promise of an endless chain of generations yet to be born.

The very subject of a bed can itself inspire an artistic treatment. Countess Joy de Rohan Chabot has played with fantasy and illusion in her creation of an outdoor trompe l'oeil bedroom complete with wafting drapery and painted bed linens. With their "Dream Bed" of branches, Elizabeth Garouste and Mattia Bonetti prompt associations with the cradle

the Italian farmhouse home of sculptor and painter Fernando Botero is perched high on the hills of the little town of Pietrasanta, surrounded by olive trees, fig trees, and grapevines. Earthy southern scents envelope the land where Botero sculpts his vision. The bedroom, with its simple flat bed, is guarded by the artist's own bronze sculptures titled "Adam and Eve."

american
artist Claes Oldenburg
created this setting titled
"Bedroom Ensemble" circa
1963 with wood, vinyl,
metal, artificial fur,
cloth, and paper. Courtesy
of National Gallery of
Canada, Ottawa.

rocking, waiting for the moment "when the bough breaks"—and the dreaming begins.

Since ancient times, kings and emperors have enlisted the talents of artists to create ideal beds, beds that are more sculpture than furniture. Such commissioned beds are a tradition that continues today. Then there are

the artists who, from a personal fascination with beds and all the associations they evoke, have created beds specifically as works of art. Alexander Calder, Max Ernst, Claes Oldenburg, and Robert Rauschenberg have each developed a singular statement of their style around bedframes, artworks that create an in-

teresting dialogue with the more familiar works of their oeuvre.

Every mind must take its rest. Whatever the bed we rest our head on, transformed as it is during the course of our mind's nighttime adventures, there is consolation in returning to the bed as we wake, with a stomach roused by an appetite for more life.

the surrealist artist Max Ernst created this "Cage Bed and Screen" circa 1974, where the sleeping space becomes the inspiration for an entire magical world. Courtesy the Lannan Foundation, Los Angeles, California, left. Photo by Barry Kinsella.

Created by Robert Rauschenberg, "Bed" (1955), is a combine painting: oil and pencil on pillow, quilt, sheet, on wood support, above.

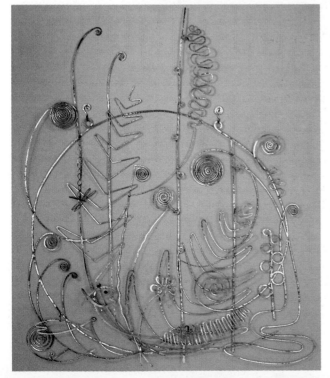

In this silver bedhead designed by Alexander Calder in the winter of 1945–1946, a characteristic energy is evident among the fish, flowers, and dragonflies hidden in its active lines. Courtesy Peggy Guggenheim Collection of Venice, left. Photo by David Heald.

the bed of artist/painter Cesar in
Provence is a design created around the
whimsical butterfly headboard. Inlaid
into the wall with fragments of mirrors,
porcelain, and glass, it commands the
setting with sparkle. Neutral colors and
open wall space make the bed the
room's artistic centerpiece, above.

"**d**ream Bed" is the title of this oak
and bronze frame created by Elizabeth
Garouste and Mattia Bonetti, circa 1990.
Its treelike lines are matched with a
plush silk sauvage bedspread suggesting
a rich earthen cushion. Courtesy Neotu
Gallery. Photo by Karine Kndslicht.

the bedroom of artist Izhar Patkin is a study in varying shades of cool blue with white columns. A simple wooden-frame bed is flanked by a matching desk. This is truly an artist's bedroom, styled with simplicity.

artist Kenny Scharf's dramatic artwork highlights his gold-washed bedroom design with its wrought iron bed. The pinwheel wrought iron's graceful, swirled form matches the corner chair in elegant tandem. Sunny ochre walls with painted stripes are bright and dazzling, right.

the children's bedroom and play area in Kenny Scharf's home is a vibrant, toy-filled treasure house with a bunk bed to climb and explore, and a crib painted by the artist with his animated outer space creatures. Fantastic shapes and colors enchant the eye with the humor and imagination of a treasured storybook, far right, above and below.

he home of designer Jacques Grange in Paris was once the apartment of one of this century's most famous women writers, Colette. The mercurial author of such gems as Gigi and Claudine once dreamed away the days and wrote away the nights in this setting. Her artistic spirit was maintained when Grange decorated the apartment as an homage to the author. An eighteenth-century sculptured steel-frame bed commands the room, while the bedroom window overlooks the gracious garden of the Palais Royal. On the cabinet, surveying the present life of her past, is a photo of Colette herself.

n writer Umberto Pasti's home, this bedroom's look and style includes a simple wrought iron–frame Roman bed from the end of the eighteenth century. A rope chair of gilded wood is from France, 1986, while the table is of Victorian wrought iron. Hanging rug tapestries and small pieces of artwork adorn the corner near the bed. The large painting is by Julian Schnabel. The striped bedcover is from Tethau, in wool. Light wood tones and burnt oranges are warm and striking.

Countess Joy de Rohan Chabot has created a complete trompe l'oeil environment for her design of this bed, with rich, glorious colors that are luxurious and inviting. The beautiful baldaquin bed is painted with blues and aubergine, gold and yellows, and crushed raspberry. A light breeze seems to blow forever through the painted drapes, and an invincible dove perches safely atop a tiny cat's house. The bed is resting on a carpet created by Flipo. On the side tables, turn-of-the-century ceramic flowerpots, signed Delfa Massie, offer a bounty of forsythia flowers and conniassier from Japan. This is truly a setting for a storybook princess.

In the Paris working loft and showroom of French designer Andrée Putman, thousands of years of history coalesce around a simple chaise longue. Surrounding the turn-of-the-century colonial Indian chaise are a 2000 BC Egyptian jackal from the Serit period, an eighteenth-century wrought iron stand, a 1920 sculptured glove by Nadja, a 1930 carpet from Eileen Gray, a 1930s polished-iron table by Pierre Chareau, a personal address book from Hermès, a cashmere blanket, a 1984 table on wheels designed for New York's Morgan's Hotel, a 1988 painting in the background by Ouattara, and a 1989 ashtray from L'Hôtel in Paris. An eclectic combination of many periods and histories placed next to each other creates an unusual and fascinating style.

This fifteenth-century Italian bed was introduced to the Villa Medici by the artist/painter Balthus when he took up residence there. With its white-curtained enclosure, it provides complete and soothing privacy. Marbleized and painted gold posters and a matching chair add a touch of the ancient past and high Renaissance style to the bed's more modern simplicity.

the splendor of the age from which this Roman couch originates is preserved in the rich color and imagery of a surrounding fresco, (cubiencum nocturnum) in the villa of P. Fanning Synistor. Courtesy of the Metropolitan Museum of Art, Rogers Fund, 1903. Photo by Schecter Lee.

Beds Throughout History and Time

Chapter 5

The first bed in the Western world was made from the trunk of an olive tree, with bright red-painted oxhide thongs strung across it to make a pliable surface. Or, at least, that is how Homer described the way Odysseus made his own bed in the time before there was history. In fact, Odysseus' bed, inlaid with precious metals, was already an advanced and ornate device for sleeping, a forerunner of later efforts to make of the bed something both beautiful and comfortable, precious and intimate, imposing and private. By definition, the bed must be different from a mere place to sleep—a pile of straw, a thickness of leaves, a reed mat—placed on the floor. The bed has to be a structure, something elevated from the ground, a raised platform, usually with legs and decoration of some sort, an opportunity for design and such crafts as textile weaving, woodcarving, jewelry, and metalworking.

The records indicate that the earliest bed, even earlier than that of Odysseus, was almost surely Egyptian, dating from the First Dynasty roughly five thousand years ago. It consisted of a rectangular framework of wooden staves perched on four carved wooden lion's legs, all facing the same direction as if it were a strange animal walking somewhere. Many of these beds have been found in Egyptian tombs. They are made of cedarwood, built to be slightly higher at the head than at the foot, and often covered with plaited leather thongs.

These beds of antiquity served several purposes besides sleep. The Egyptians used them as funeral biers, thus making the bed synonymous with all of life, from beginning to end. Many peoples, including the ancient Hebrews, ate lying down, so the bed served as a dining place as well as a sleeping place. This custom seems to have been copied by the Greeks, who passed it on to the Etruscans and the Romans. These early beds are pictured on Greek vases. They were very tall and they were climbed into with the help of a separate platform.

The bed developed also in Asia. In China, as in Europe during the Middle Ages, it came to be a kind of room-within-a-room, an autonomous, closed structure providing a cozy, protected, intimate place in the middle of a room. The Chinese bed had four posts supporting a thick wooden canopy that was itself draped in silk brocade or some other textile. This complete house-inside-a-house came with a little antechamber

in the form of a ve-
randa. Surprisingly per-
haps, the Chinese bed
was close to the basic
design used in Europe
for many centuries.
Throughout the Middle
Ages and well into the
Renaissance, the four-
poster bed, made in
several different ways,
was most common. One
type was tentlike; the
bed was covered entirely
by drapery and curtains
and placed in the center
of the room in a period
when houses were badly
heated and drafty and
when the importance of
fresh air was not appre-
ciated. The bed became
a small unit of habita-
tion, an ornate, refined,
and beautifully created
substitute for the larger
house itself.

In the seventeenth
and eighteenth centu-
ries, the time of absolute
monarchies in Europe,
the bedchamber be-
came a center of courtly
life. Beds were enor-
mous and highly deco-
rated four-posters whose
wooden framework was
entirely covered in tex-
tile. The bed of the

this Tuscan bed from the Italian Renaissance is a reminder of an era rich in artistry and craftsmanship. Opulent details dazzle the eye and are a reminder of a past that is filled with both beauty and mystery. Private collection, left.

although this bed was carved in the French Renaissance, its most famous owners belong to our time. Now belonging to HRH Prince Michael of Greece, a distant aunt, Queen Marie of Romania, was crazy about it. She was a famous beauty whose memoirs read like a novel. Before this, the bed was owned by author Sir Arthur Conan Doyle, who penned the celebrated tales of Sherlock Holmes, right.

Pastel colors and details like those of an ancient fresco are found in "The Bacchus Room" at Villa Foscari, La Malcontenta, near Venice. The four-poster Italian Renaissance baldaquin bed stands under a restored fifteenth-century fresco depicting allegorical scenes in an imaginary garden, left.

a bed from the time of the Sun King graces this room. It originally belonged to Madame de Maintenon, Louis XIV's mistress and the governess of his children. She founded the School of Saint-Cyr, a finishing school for noble young ladies. The tapestry and bedcover in petit point were both created by the desmoiselles of the school using biblical scenes as the design's theme. The bed's history followed the map of Europe; it was sold and sent to Italy, then to Ireland and England, finally returning to France, where it now stands majestically, left.

It is here, in a setting both opulent and bold, that the "Sun King" Louis XIV took his rest in the royal apartments at the Château de Versailles. It is majestically draped with heavy gold-thread brocade and topped by four fountains of white ostrich plumes emphasizing the bed's dramatic height, right.

monarch was the primary bed of the kingdom, as evidenced by the *levée du roi*, attended by all the princes of the blood, the dukes, and the important courtiers living in the palace. One pulled aside the king's heavy bed curtain, another held up the royal dressing gown, another put the royal slippers on the royal feet. A new day at court had begun.

During this entire epoch, fine craftsmen transformed the bed into a product of the highest artistic refinement, creating canopies in imitation of church steeples, ornately carved posts, and frames embedded with statues and adorned with pillars. Often the wood was lacquered or gilded. These beds of the wealthy were huge; the largest one known to us today occupied a room in the Crown Inn in the English town of Ware and is known, naturally enough, as the Great Bed of Ware. Made in the Tudor period, it was about twelve feet by twelve feet and is mentioned by Shakespeare in *Twelfth Night*. Legend has it that entire groups of men and women passed the night in it in happy intimacy.

These beds of the great houses, the aristocracy, and the rising commercial classes re-

a *hâteau de Haroué in the Lorraine Valley, France, the home of Princess Minnie de Beauvau-Craon, has a room in which one can walk through time. The stately seventeenth-century canopy bed sets the tone in this grand receiving chamber. The antique crimson drapes are embroidered with the insignia "Ave Maria."*

the Paris residence of Karl Lagerfeld is done in grand style with a magnificent Louis XV bed by Delanois, circa 1760. The gold-leaf-painted wood frame is draped with lustrous royal blue velvet, tied to the side by tassels of gold thread. Ostrich feathers dome the cupola. The silk factories of Lyons created the fabrics, prepared from documentary research of the originals. The period style is well respected in this room of pure elegance.

flected a major evolution in private life: the creation of separate zones in the house reserved for bedtime activities—for love, sleep, birth, and death. Until the seventeenth century, the beds of the wealthy were placed usually in the middle of the room, but later, reflecting the growing attachment to privacy, the sleeping alcove, borrowed from Spain, became common. Beds became smaller, designed no longer as entire microhouses, but as places just big enough for one person or a couple to sleep. In more modest homes—convents, monasteries, and peasant dwellings—the bed, a far simpler affair, was still placed in the room where other activities were carried out. The bed in the monastic cell was placed in a kind of armoire along a wall, hidden during the day by wooden panels. The typical farmhouse bed, unadorned by rich tapestries and curtains, was placed in an alcove,

often in the kitchen, where it would be protected from drafts.

The Empire period in France, dominated by Napoleon, brought about the first major change in the form of the bed in several centuries. Inspired by the design of the Roman couch, known from excavations in Pompeii and Herculaneum, it had a very high frame whose two ends consisted of spiral supports. It was covered with a tentlike structure and was given a martial look by the spears that held up the curtains or drapes. But the bed went through other fads and fashions. At the time of the French Revolution, for example, there were the "patriotic beds" whose posts were surmounted by Phrygian bonnets, one of the main revolutionary symbols. The bed of the empress Josephine followed an Egyptian model, in commemoration of Napoleon's conquest of Egypt in the beginning of the nine-

the history and the passions of the royals are remembered in this bed of France's most famous queen, Marie Antoinette. Married to Louis XVI, she bore witness to her country's greatest upheavals and changes. But before revolution came to France, the queen slept in this opulent bed at the Château de Fontainebleau with its rich brocade and gilt-touch headboard.

teenth century. The painter Jacques-Louis David designed the bed *en bateau*, that is, in the form of a boat, a style that remained popular for much of the first half of the nineteenth century. The canopy was held up by a kind of

mast and the frame was curved to make it look like a seafaring vessel. One bed *en bateau*, included in a book of bed designs in 1827, was in the form of a Venetian gondola. Others were decorated with allegorical bronze figures or

encrusted with enamel cameos, their canopies adorned with crowns of sculpted poppies gilded and surmounted with white feathers.

It was during the middle of the nineteenth century that the bed took on the form it has

today, becoming more functional, less ceremonially decorated, and more adapted to the modern house. One technical innovation was the iron-frame bed first used in hospitals in the middle of the nineteenth century but later

this Italian eighteenth-century bed belongs to the collection of Frederick P. Victoria. The luxury of its heavy engraved frame is a striking contrast with the simplicity of the bed's open-frame design. The bed is covered with antique bedsheets and pillows. A sunflower decorates its headboard, and a beautiful carved jug rests at the foot.

In the Paris residence of the Count and Countess Brando Brandolini D'Adda is a guest room whose French eighteenth-century lit à la Dubarry is upholstered in yellow and gold brocade. With gilded wood and opulent detail, this lavish room steps gracefully out of the past.

becoming a bed for the home. Another technological step came with the invention of the metal spring mattress, which is more hygienic, more practical, and more resistant to parasites than traditional mattresses. Rooms became smaller and so did the beds. Canopies disappeared, usually leaving just the bed's bare structure—the four posts, connected at the top by a simple rectangular frame; and the headboards and footboards, carved of wood or made of iron covered with papier-mâché. As time went by, the bed became simpler still. The frame sometimes disappeared altogether, leaving just the headboard and the footboard that one sees today.

But though the beds themselves are simpler, new refinements have been added to bedclothes, mattresses, and pillows, making them more comfortable and practical while still highly decorative. Further, the bed has taken

*t*he campaign bed of Napoleon I at Château de Compiègne was both a place to rest and the imperial military headquarters of the brilliant general. Utilitarian yet aesthetic, its nomadic tent was easily transported to the next scene of conquest Courtesy of Musée Napoléon, Château de Fontainebleau.

*t*he emperor Napoleon's bedroom at Compiègne is a study in masculine opulence. Rich, deep crimson dominates the room's mood. Golden leaves and stars are a touch of military prestige and power.

napoleon I's room at Malmaison combines the look of a military headquarters with a simple, almost austere imperial style. The nomadic desert tones of the flowing draperies create a sense of temporary encampment. A Winged Victory stands in the center of the room as a reminder of its owner's glory and power.

on the character of various schools of architecture. In America there are Colonial beds, Shaker beds, and Quaker beds. In the West Indies there are simple four-poster beds with highly polished ebony frames. Each decorative style fosters its own style of bed—art nouveau beds, simple Bauhaus beds, art deco beds, and others. With the turn of the century, design took a giant step. But the basic form and function remain consistent with the values of modern life. The bed, most important of all, has entered entirely into the realm of private life. Reserved for the most intimate parts of the home and for life's most intimate moments, the bed is an exclusive zone of contemplation, tenderness, love, sickness, recuperation, death—all the aspects of life that require a protected, safe, and comfortable place walled off from the noise and the interference of our public spaces.

the passions of the imperials are brought to life in the empress Marie-Louise's bedroom in the Château de Compiègne. This is the most lavish and ornate room in the residence, with decor designed by Bertault. The bed itself is an august masterpiece created by Jacob Desmalter. Topped by a gilded crown, the draperies are hand-held by two winged guards sculpted in gilded wood.

the formal luxury of the empress Josephine's palace life at Fontainebleau is recalled with the beauty of her imperial bed, a lit à l'Oriental. Its beaded canopy hangs like a monarchic headdress. This design reflects elegance and restraint, with classic, neutral colors of dignified simplicity.

the life and story of the empress Josephine are evoked by her bed at Malmaison. Designed by Jacob Desmalter, its drapery flows from a royal crown to the golden swans below, which were the empress's insignia. An eagle standing on the crown supports the draperies. Divorced from Napoleon in 1809, the empress died in this bed, May 29, 1814.

married to Napoleon III, the empress Eugénie resided in majestic splendor at Compiègne with a touch of rococo opulence. A highly detailed canopy is topped by winged cherubs bearing the empress's imperial initial, left.

king Louis XVIII slept in this magnificent bed at the Château de Haroué, France. With a classic boat shape, it is made of acajou wood and decorated with gilded bronze poppy buds ornamenting each of its corners. It is dressed with a silk bedcover and antique white linens, bottom right.

"**a**ll my wishes end where I hope my days will end...at Monticello," Thomas Jefferson said of his magnificent home in Virginia's Blue Ridge Mountains. Jefferson was inspired by English and French styling, to which he was frequently exposed in his travels. In this early-nineteenth-century alcove bed, he established an interesting mixture of seclusion and openness. Beyond the bed lies his study, where he conducted much of his private life and intellectual pursuits, left. Courtesy Thomas Jefferson Memorial Foundation. Photo by Hal Conroy.

art collector Paul Anduy's bedroom near Paris contains a fin de siècle bed by Bellery Desfontaines. Turn-of-the-century style is expressed in the detailed oak headboard, while the approach of the modern age is signaled with the twentieth-century design. The headboard depicts carved gold-leaf apples, one of which can be removed; it is inscribed with the names of the family members. This bed marks the passing of one age and the commencement of another, right and below.

ringed on its frame, headboard, and matching nightstand with inlaid wood poppies, a suggestion of the altered dream state of consciousness, this Louis Majorelle bed was surrounded with the visions of classic paintings of Lucy Anduy, a nineteenth-century art collector, right.

this orchestration of rosewood, Cuban mahogany, and various other inlaid woods around a decorative motif of ormolu water-lily mounts is one of the finest examples of the work of French designer Louis Majorelle. A remarkable piece of craftsmanship, it was created at the turn of the century, reputedly for the mistress of the kaiser's son, the crown prince of Germany. Today, it is housed in the Virginia Museum of Fine Arts.

Created by Emile-Jacques Ruhlmann and entitled "Sun Bed," this is a French design dating from 1930. A starburst of texture and shape, it is constructed from Macassar ebony and has a white-oak base and a luminous cellulose finish. The remarkable headboard dominates the entire piece with its effect of a solar eclipse. Originally designed for French actress Jane Renouardt, it now resides in the Virginia Museum of Fine Arts.

the settled and utilitarian air of the 1950s breathes through this Milano bedroom. Uncomplicated and basic, its unadorned simplicity is reflective of a decade in which people returned to clarity after the turbulence of the modern age's first fifty years.

Dream Beds

We climb into bed, enveloped by fresh sheets; the head falls to the pillow and the body stretches out across the mattress. This is the way we abandon ourselves to sleep...letting go of the alert body, sacrificing the logical mind for the fantastical.

The bed's invitation is irresistible: one can never escape the need to sleep for long. Sooner or later, the deep pull of this natural cycle wins out and we succumb. It is as natural as the sun and the moon, the cycle of the seasons, life and death.

The god of dreams in Greek mythology, Morpheus, was born of the god of sleep, Hypnos. A twin brother was born with Hypnos, the god of death, Thanatos. Their father was god of the night. In a dream, it seems everything falls into place.

From the early years of life, the bed is a place for fantasy. It is all but impossible for a child to fall asleep without first hearing a bedtime story. As the words unfold, wondrous visions take shape, surrounding this young mind in a soft cushion of the imaginary, protection from the harsh world of the real. Step by step, the child is led safely into the uncontrolled world of dreaming. Bedtime stories, the creations of minds like Hans Christian Andersen and the Brothers Grimm, have a special quality, meant as they were to be heard in this strange pocket between waking and

romance and mystery create a seductively alluring chemistry in this roomful of reflections. An elegant chandelier's crystalline refractions, the fragile light of candles, and the mirrored illusion of space set the atmosphere for an inspired tête-à-tête in this artist's studio in the Paris residence of Loulou de la Falaise and her husband, Thadée Klossowski. The bed is an American Louis XV–style lit à cross, given to Loulou by her mother, Maxime de la Falaise. Upholstered in pear-green velvet, this daybed is dressed with antique pillows and blankets, and bedsheets trimmed with exquisite lace by Agnès Comar. This baroque and feminine setting normally provides a sitting space, and occasionally a bed for a friend...but it is one that invites the passions to let themselves be known.

an aesthetic fantasy surrounds this Indo-Portuguese bed, set in a room walled with flamboyant gold leaf motifs in the Château de Haroué, the home of Princess Minnie de Beauvau-Craon in the province of Lorraine, France. There is an air of the exotic to this bed, decorated with a peacock head at each of its corners. A royal family insignia crowns the headboard, and an antique silk bedcover keeps warm the history held hidden within it.

dreaming. Dorothy's journey through the magical land of Oz took place, the story goes, entirely in a dream. In "Briar Rose," more familiar to us as "Sleeping Beauty," a young maiden wakes from her slumber to find herself living a dream come true.

Once past the age for such stories, preparing to retire to the bed may require a different kind of lulling and the familiarity of a relaxing bedtime routine. It may involve nothing more than escaping the day-time clothes, a skin to be shed. Or it may include a soothing cup of tea, or warm milk, brushing the teeth or the hair, or perhaps putting on a comforting nightgown or favorite pair of pajamas. These are the bedtime rituals that compensate for the bedtime stories we no longer hear.

Every sleeper dreams. Some may not recall these odd rearrangements of the real world upon awakening. But during the night, the body experiences brief periods in which sleep is at its deepest. These intervals, fifteen or twenty minutes long, are known as REM (Rapid Eye Movement) sleep, so named for the characteristic darting movements of the eyes under their closed lids. A particular brain-wave pattern occurs, and from random electrical impulses occurring in the nerve cells in the cortex area of the brain, the images of dreams are born.

For as long as time has been recorded, dreams have been valued as a realm of privileged insight, revealing truths we might otherwise fail to see. Ancient—and not so ancient—leaders would often make key decisions regarding the fate of their country based on dreams. Sigmund Freud attempted to elevate the interpretation of dreams to a science, mapping our internal world of unconscious memories and desires, and Carl Jung followed in his path. Abraham Lincoln was said to have witnessed his own assassination

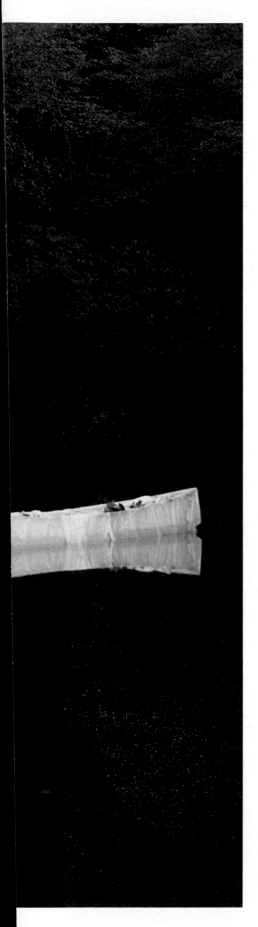

one night in a dream.

Sometimes, we will waken in the dark from an especially remarkable dream, compelled to reflect on it. We might switch on the bedside light and scratch out some notes with pencil and paper, hoping that in daylight we will be able to decipher the message it hides. Somehow, we feel it might mean everything; and yet we know it might mean nothing at all. This uncertainty fascinated many writers, as

has the entire phenomenon of sleep. Shakespeare, Emily Dickinson, Tennyson, T. S. Eliot…like us, they slept and dreamed, and were awed by it.

In a dream, we might find the world beyond the edges of our bed transformed into an orchard, or a strange cavern, or the sand beside a roaring ocean. While the destination will rarely be known, the bed is always our vehicle… and it can transport us to many fantastical places.

It is a very special hour— awakening to the dawn in the lush colors and fragrances of the forest. A twig bed, embraced by vines at the side of the lake, is a candle-lit vision that evokes the fabled wonder of Sleeping Beauty. It is the bed of Diane Von Furstenberg's daughter Tatiana, decorated by Konstantine Kakanias with a cloudlike gathering of bedcovers and white linens hand-painted with delicate ivy leaves, above and left.

this room is found in the New York City apartment of art expert Thilo von Watzdorf. Against the bottle-green lacquered bedroom walls, the sumptuous ormolu and mahogany bed is flanked by two gold-leaf sculpted guardian angels. It is thought to have been designed by Charles Percier, Napoleon Bonaparte's architect, for the eccentric William Beckford, at one time the richest man in England, right and below.

a *simple couch timelessly waits for its audience to arrive and a theatrical fantasy to begin. This charming theater in a private residence outside of Venice is a place where privileged guests and family members might gather after a wonderful dinner to enjoy a shared dream: perhaps a commedia dell'arte chamber piece, populated by the likes of Pulchinella, Colombina, and Pantalone. A backdrop designed by Lila de Nobile provides the setting on a stage bordered on either side by two private loggias of pink and white stucco.*

diane Von Furstenberg's home in Connecticut is an escape from the city. A hammock draped with embroidered white antique linens and soft pillows sways in the afternoon breeze. An old-fashioned barn can be seen as the sun breaks through the heavily greened trees in this country setting.

by a lamppost, at the edge of the lapping waters of the Seine in Paris, this poetic scene is a gentle pocket of private reflection, forever escaping the pull of Parisian city time. A turn-of-the-century camp bed rests on the tip of the Ile St.-Louis, warmed by a book and a bottle of wine.

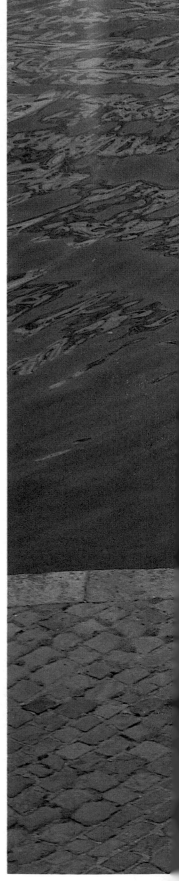

Carried off in our
dreams to the vast luxury
of sleep, we relish the
soft silence of the pillow,
riding to nowhere and
leaving behind only the
frothing blue-green waters
of the Mediterranean Sea.
This creates the sublime ideal
of sleep between acres
of sea and a brilliant sky.
Photographed by Antoine
Meyer and styled by
Geraldine Grinda.

"So I
awoke,
and behold
it was
a dream."

John Bunhyan

Sources

Linens

AD HOC SOFTWARES
410 West Broadway
New York, NY 10012

AGNÈS COMAR LINEN
7 Avenue Georges V
Paris 75008

ANN JACOB AMERICA
Antiques
756 Madison Avenue
New York, NY 10021

AU CHAT BOTTÉ BOUTIQUE
903 Madison Avenue
New York, NY 10021

CHRISTIAN BENAIS
ANTIQUE LINEN
18 Rue Cortanbert
Paris 75016

DESCAMPS
454 Columbus Avenue
New York, NY 10024

THE DOWN COMPANY
673 Madison Avenue
New York, NY 10021

DOWN QUILT SHOP
518 Columbus Avenue
New York, NY 10024

D'PORTHAULT & CO.
18 East 69th Street
New York, NY 10021

E. BRAUN LINENS LTD.
717 Madison Avenue
New York, NY 10021

FIVE-EGGS
436 West Broadway
New York, NY 10012

FRETTE LINEN
787 Madison Avenue
New York, NY 10021

JESURUM LINEN
Ponte Canonica 4310
Venezia, Italy

KELTER-MALCE
Antique American Quilts
and Indian Blankets
361 Bleecker Street
New York, NY 10014

LERON, INC., LINEN
750 Madison Avenue
New York, NY 10021

MANUEL CANOVAS BOUTIQUE
5 Place Furstenberg
Paris 75006

NOËL LINEN
49 Avenue Montaigne
Paris 75008

PRATESI LINENS
829 Madison Avenue
New York, NY 10021

SCHWEITZER LINENS
457 Columbus Avenue
New York, NY 10024

SHERIDAN
595 Madison Avenue
New York, NY 10021

THOS. K. WOODARD
American Antiques
and Quilts
835 Madison Avenue
New York, NY 10021

Antiques

ANNE-SOPHIE DUVAL
Antiques
5 Quai Malaquais
75006 Paris

C. T. LOO ASIAN ART
48 Rue de Courcelle
Paris 75008

GABRIELLE LAROCHE
Moyen Age
Renaissance XVII
12 Rue de Beaune
Paris 75007

GIANFRANCO LUZZETTI
Antichita
Borgo S. Jacopo 28-A
50125 Firenze, Italy

L'ILE DU DEMONT
Primitive Art
13 Rue Bonaparte
Paris 75006

MADELEINE CASTAING
ANTIQUES
21 Rue Bonaparte
Paris 75006

MARCEL GRUNSPAN
Antiques
6 & 8 Rue Royale
Paris 75008

NICOLE ALTERO
Antiques
21 Quai Voltaire
Paris 75007

Furniture

ALICE'S ANTIQUES
552 Columbus Avenue
New York, NY 10024

FREDERICK P. VICTORIA
AND SON
Antiques, Architectural
Interiors
154 East 55th Street
New York, NY 10022

JOHANNA SEITZ
Southwestern Furniture
44 Main Street, Rt 45
New Preston, CT 06777

KYOTO ARTS AND FASHIONS
927 Madison Avenue
New York, NY 10021

PHILIP COLLECK
OF LONDON
Antique English Furniture
and Works of Art
630 Broadway
New York, NY 10003

PORTICO
American Furniture
379 West Broadway
New York, NY 10012

ROBERT HOMMA
WILLIAM LIPTON
27 East 61 Street
New York, NY 10021